WHAT'S INSIDE ME?

My BONES

by Rachel Rose

BEARPORT
PUBLISHING

Minneapolis, Minnesota

Credits: Cover, all background © Piotr Urakau/Shutterstock; cover, 7, 23 © BlueRingMedia/Shutterstock, cover, 4, 10, 14, 16, 21, 22 bones illustration © Shutterstock; 4 Sergey Novikov/Shutterstock; 5 Samuel Borges Photography/Shutterstock; 4 Robert Kneschke/Shutterstock; 5 Sergey Novikov/Shutterstock; 6 Zoia Kostina/Shutterstock; 7 (skeleton illustrations) KamimiArt/Shutterstock; 8 svtdesign/Shutterstock; 9 Art of Kosi/Shutterstock; 10 wavebreakmedia/Shutterstock; 11 kentoh/Shutterstock; 12 MDGRPHCS/Shutterstock; 13T Matis75/Shutterstock; 13B Lightspring/Shutterstock; 14L Asia Images Group/Shutterstock; 14R vystekimages/Shutterstock; 15 Jihan Nafiaa Zahri/Shutterstock; 16/17 EreborMountain/Shutterstock; 18 LightField Studios/Shutterstock; 19 Tatjana Baibakova/Shutterstock; 20 Iakov Filimonov/Shutterstock; 21 Pixel-Shot/Shutterstock.

President: Jen Jenson
Director of Product Development: Spencer Brinker
Senior Editor: Allison Juda
Associate Editor: Charly Haley
Designer: Oscar Norman

Library of Congress Cataloging-in-Publication Data is available at www.loc.gov or upon request from the publisher.

ISBN: 978-1-63691-440-4 (hardcover)
ISBN: 978-1-63691-447-3 (paperback)
ISBN: 978-1-63691-454-1 (ebook)

Copyright © 2022 Bearport Publishing Company. All rights reserved. No part of this publication may be reproduced in whole or in part, stored in any retrieval system, or transmitted in any form or by any means, electronic, mechanical, photocopying, recording, or otherwise, without written permission from the publisher.

For more information, write to Bearport Publishing, 5357 Penn Avenue South, Minneapolis, MN 55419. Printed in the United States of America.

CONTENTS

The Inside Scoop 4
Let's Connect 6
Bony Shapes 8
Stand Tall 10
Safety First 12
Teamwork 14
Living Bones 16
Strong Bones 18
Keep On Movin' 20
Your Busy Body 22
Glossary 24
Index 24

THE INSIDE SCOOP

Your body is a super machine that keeps you moving, learning, and having fun. But how does it work? The secret is inside!

I'll hold you up!

When you sit up straight, your bones are hard at work. Without your bones, you would flop to the floor. Let's take a closer look.

LET'S CONNECT

Bones are all over your body. In fact, you had about 300 of them when you were born. They are the frame for everything else.

Some bones come together as you grow. You end up with 206.

BONY SHAPES

Bones come in different shapes and sizes. Many bones in your head are flat. Other bones are round, such as the ones in your back. A bone in your knee is shaped like a triangle.

What did you say?

A bone in your ear is about the size of a grain of rice!

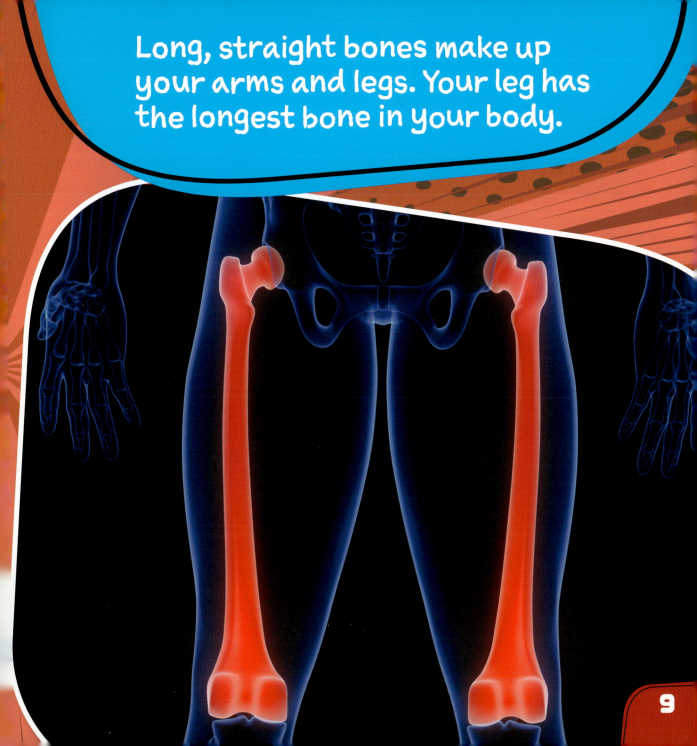
Long, straight bones make up your arms and legs. Your leg has the longest bone in your body.

STAND TALL

One of the skeleton's big jobs is to give you **support**. It holds you up.

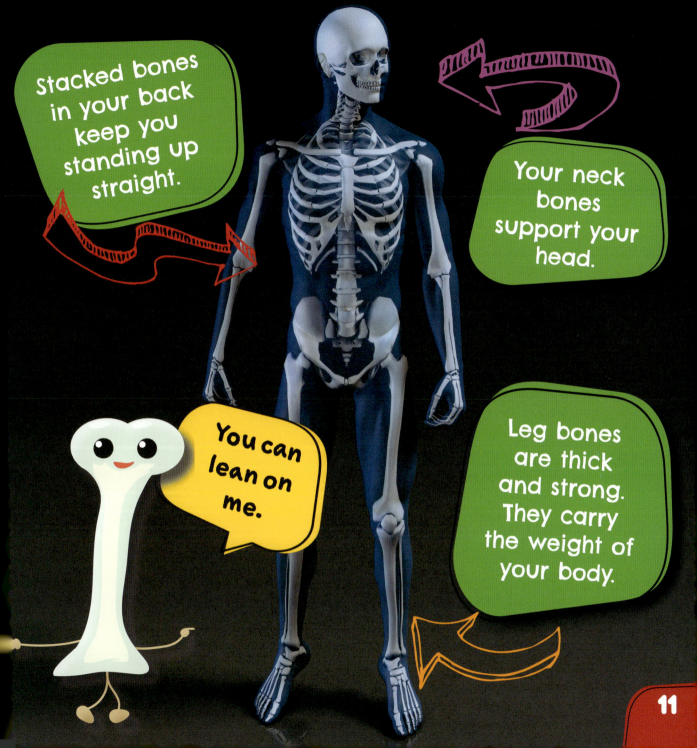

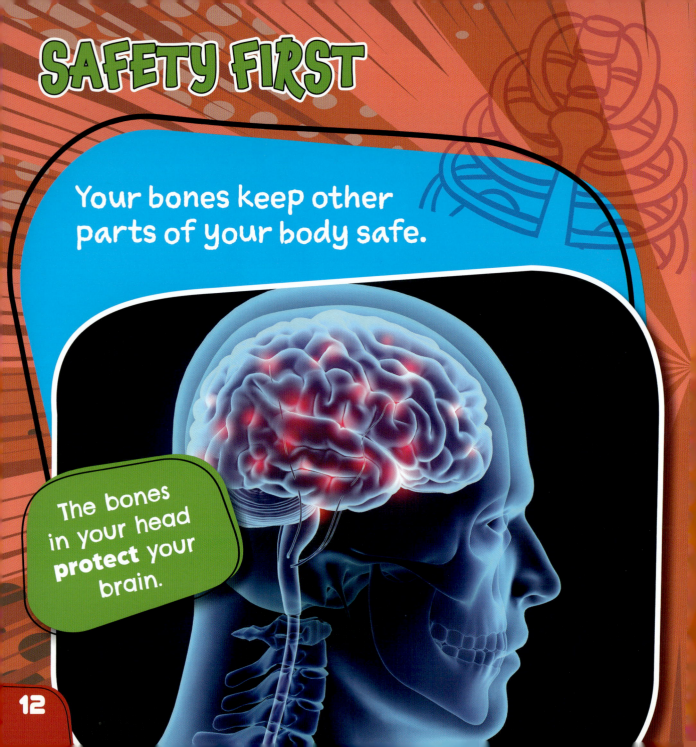

SAFETY FIRST

Your bones keep other parts of your body safe.

The bones in your head **protect** your brain.

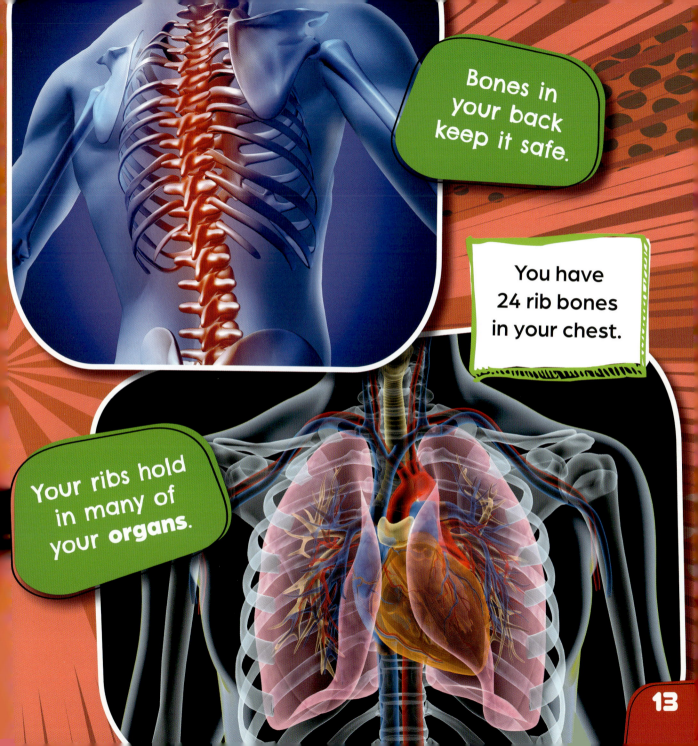

Teamwork

Your bones would not be able to move if they didn't have some help. **Joints** let you bend and move where two bones meet.

Some joints move in all directions. You can wiggle your shoulders and hips!

Some move forward and backward. Try bending your elbows and knees.

LIVING BONES

Even though bones need help to move, they are alive. Bones have **layers**. And each part is living.

The outer layer is thin.

When a bone breaks, it can fix itself!

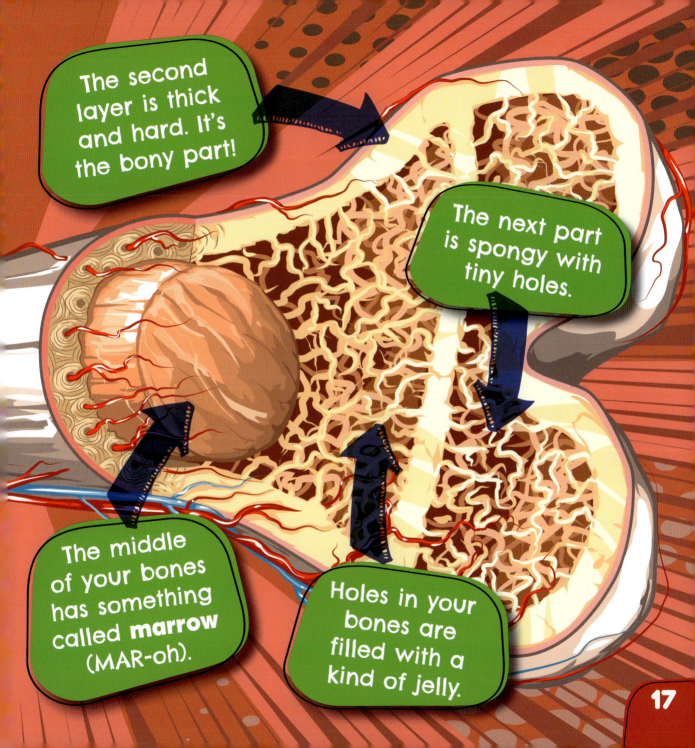

STRONG BONES

As your bones grow, so do you. It's important to give your bones the right foods so they will grow strong.

Your bones need **calcium**. It keeps them healthy. There is calcium in milk, cheese, and nuts. Some fruits and veggies have it, too!

KEEP ON MOVIN'

Exercise is good for your bones. Kick a ball around or dance with your friends to get your body moving. There are many fun ways to exercise!

YOUR BUSY BODY

Your bones are an important part of the super machine that is your body. They work with lots of other things inside you. Together, they keep you going every day!

It's what's inside that counts.

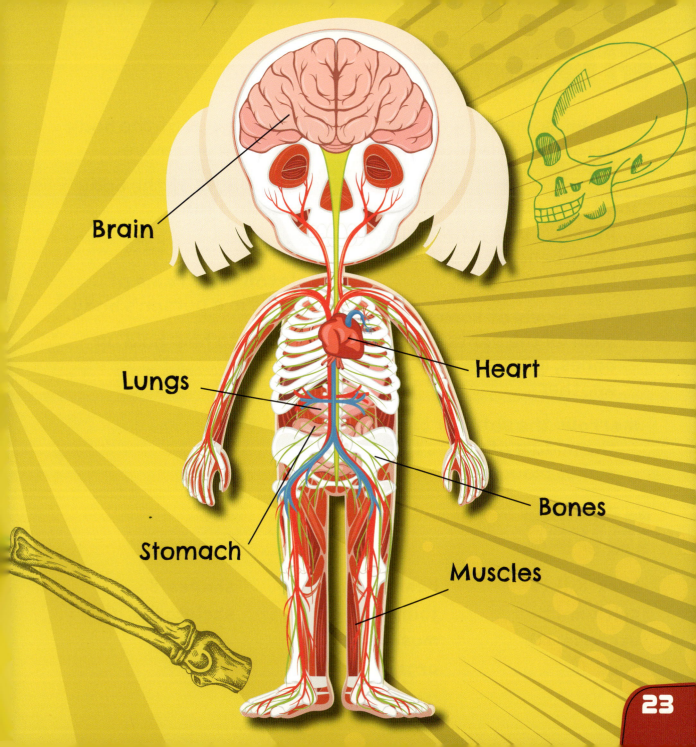

GLOSSARY

calcium something found in food that is good for bones

joints the parts in a person's body that help them bend where two bones meet

layers levels of something, such as the parts of bones, lying one over another

marrow the soft part in the middle of bones that makes blood

muscles parts of the body that help you move

organs parts of the body that do a job

protect to keep safe

skeleton the frame of bones in a person's body

support to help hold up

INDEX

back 8, 11, 13
calcium 19
exercise 20
food 18
head 7–8, 11–12
joints 14–15
muscles 15, 23
organs 13
shapes 8
skeleton 7, 10